WINNING THE JOB HUNT

by

John Parsons

Table of Contents

Introduction 1

Starting Out on the Job Hunt 3

Where Do You Start! Developing a Strategy 6

The Résumé 8

Shall I send a Cover Letter? 32

The Phone Interview 34

The Interview 37

Behavioural Descriptive Interviews 41

Dress For Success and To Impress 45

The Untold Truth About Interviews… 48

Dealing With Why You Left Your Last Job 50

Social Media and the Job Hunt 52

Twitter 59

The Follow Up 61

Wrapping It Up 64

Introduction

I am passionate about helping Job Seekers. Getting a job for many can be life changing. For others it ensures they can take care of their families or save to go back to school. This passion eventually led me to create and launch an incredibly successful Staffing and Recruitment agency that worked with clients all over Canada and the US; leading their talent acquisition processes and hiring thousands of employees.

I didn't start off in recruiting or Human Resources. I have had an interesting career since leaving graduate school. Officer in the Army. Consultant. Taught undergrad classes at University and local Colleges. Throughout this multi-faceted career, It is the impact of being part of a significant and important stage in the lives of others that has given me the most satisfaction.

This book is designed to help relatively new job seekers and perhaps seasoned employees who have not had to look for a job for some time. It is largely all based on my experience 'in the trenches' in both HR and Staffing Agency owner roles.

John Parsons

I try here to give a straightforward approach to helping you navigate what can often be a challenging process. I sincerely hope you will find value in the pages ahead and that maybe something will jump out and resonate with you – something you will apply – that will get you the job offer you've been waiting for.

Happy Reading……

Starting Out on the Job Hunt

Looking for a job. Where do I start. There is so much information out there about how you should write a résumé, how you should dress for an interview, what questions you need to ask; and that's on top of the emotional side of looking - wondering if you are qualified and questioning your abilities, needing a job to pay the bills, looking for a position that offers benefits for you and your family. It's not the easiest of times. I truly get that. I've been there too....

John Parsons

I've interviewed thousands of job seekers and read through thousands more résumés and applications. Some were great; others.......not so great. From people showing up with no shoes to others who brought in a coffee and a snack; to a candidate who rollerbladed right in to the meeting - I've seen a lot! And that is just at the interview stage! I've seen employees I've hired for clients call in sick every day after day one; a brand new employee who called me asking me to come pick him up and take him to work because his ride didn't show to a fellow who actually after the first week took off to another country without telling anyone and then called from overseas saying he will be in for his next shift - 3 weeks after he went missing!!

Now these are extreme cases and thankfully fairly rare. But in all the experience I have had in the industry there are definitely things to do and more importantly NOT to do to be successful - not only in applying but during the first critical few weeks on the job.

Whether you are a seasoned professional in your industry or more junior on the job search and employment ladder it is my hope that you will learn some tips here that will help you. If you already have a job lined up that is great. Read on though as we will be discussing some of the best practices you can use; as an employee, to succeed at your job and later, during the job search should you wish to change employers.

About Me.

I made the move to Canada over 20 years ago - way before the days of the internet and social media. Job hunting for me was hours going through newspaper ads; calling companies and perhaps typing (yes - typing on a typewriter!!) application letters.

After a few different 'careers' and more than 7 years at University everything lined up for me to the point where I eventually launched a Recruitment Agency. Over the years I have interviewed, employed and placed with employers thousands of Job Seekers including many entry level, fresh out of school employees. (Sadly schools don't seem to be preparing graduating students for the realities of the modern job market…. but that is another discussion). Through this work I have grown to understand that there is no cookie cutter approach producing a 'typical' job seeker and further; I have learned that Job Seekers can benefit from understanding; from an insider's perspective, what makes a successful job hunt and how best to start out.

I believe in getting to the heart of the matter right away; avoiding adding too much fluff and unimportant information and giving you the key, actionable information that will help you. So let's go…..

Where Do You Start! Developing a Strategy

It might sound strange but be clear about what you want to actually do! Now this might be hard for someone trying to land any job to pay bills or just to get started but try to have a real sense about the job you want. This will definitely impact your job search in so far as it will allow you to more meaningfully craft your applications and overall approach. You will save yourself a lot of time and work if you have something of a job search strategy. A few questions you might want to ask yourself first.

- What kind of job do I want? Are you looking for something to help build your background in a specific industry?

- Are you looking for anything right now to help pay the bills?

- Am I willing to relocate?

- Am I qualified for the jobs I want? Or do I have experience in lieu of formal qualifications?

- What are my salary expectations?

Getting a better sense as to What you are looking for and Why will help you narrow down your work and allow you to concentrate your efforts a little more. It will give you a better sense of which companies you want to target; who to send résumés to and how to better position yourself for the road ahead!

The Résumé

But first things first. You need to introduce yourself to companies. They need to know who you are and know that you are looking for a job. What do you need? A Résumé of course! I'm assuming you know what this is. Most job seekers I have met from around the world already have a version of a résumé but for those of you who might just be getting started or have no idea what this is - a résumé in short; is you on paper.

It might be called by various names: Resume; Résumé; CV, Curriculum Vitae….. Throughout North America this document is generally referred to as your Résumé (mostly without the accents!!) and we see CV used mostly in the UK, Europe and throughout Africa and Asia. More and more however, 'Résumé' is becoming increasingly more acceptable. There are a few subtle differences between a résumé and a CV - a CV is often a lot longer and more in depth - telling more of a life story which is in fact what *Curriculum Vitae* means in Latin – 'Life's Work'. For the rest of this book I will be referring to this document as a Résumé.

So, what exactly is a résumé? Wikipedia's definition suggests; "…*The résumé is usually one of the first items… that a potential employer encounters regarding the job seeker and is typically used to screen applicants…*"

A résumé is you on paper. It tells someone who has never met you what you have to offer. It details your work history. Tells us where you went to school and what level of academic achievement you attained. It provides details about specific work accomplishments as well as details on how to get in contact with you.

Important to note however is the use of the term 'screen…' in the definition above. It is used by the hiring manager to say "Yes - let's consider this applicant a little more..' or 'No - they are not qualified and let's move on…' Obviously, we want the first reaction! In short - your résumé, during the first stage, screens you In - or screens you Out - of the application process.

So, what does a résumé look like? Check out the example at the end of this chapter for a suggested résumé format. It works best and I will explain as we go through why this is.

In essence it is a list - although I don't want you to think of it as a simple list. Generally, in chronological order it explains what you have been doing for the past several years starting with the most recent and working backwards. How far should it go? Well - this depends on the level of experience you have; how many years of experience you have and to some degree the level of the job you are applying for. A basic rule of thumb is the last (if you have that many years of experience) 10 years. Again, this is not a hard and fast rule - more of a guideline and again, will be determined by the position you are applying for and your level of experience.

How long should your résumé be?

I've seen everything from one paragraph résumés to one that was about 12 pages long!! Definitely the first was too short and the second was way too long - I didn't have enough time in my schedule to read it! Funnily enough it came from a person who works in recruitment. He was applying to work directly for me and thought it was necessary to add every single mandate he had ever worked on for every single client. Not sure if he was trying to beat me down with details or if he actually thought this is what he needed to do! What concerned me here was that he was advising job seekers on what to do to land interviews!

How long a résumé should be is one of the most debated questions out there among industry professionals and there are no hard and fast rules. A job seeker wants to cram as much information into a résumé as possible to show they are perfect for the job and it is tempting to run on and on. I would suggest though that less is more. Many in the industry agree that once your résumé has made it through the online screening program, a recruiter may only spend about 12-15 seconds with your document. Knowing this – conciseness is definitely key!

A recent report confirms what many people might tell you - 2 pages is ideal. Not only did the majority of participants in a résumé study say they prefer 2 page résumés (between 1.4 and 2.9 times more) they also responded that they spent more time considering a 2 page résumé over a one page résumé - not only because there was more content to read but because they naturally expected to see two pages and were left feeling something was missing when given one page versions!

Whether you are a brand-new job seeker or a seasoned and highly experienced professional, the advice from experts is to attempt to present your experience and background in a two-page document.

Keep in mind though - if you are a brand-new job seeker with very limited; if any, experience - one page may work for you.

Presenting yourself over two pages can be difficult for both the new job seeker and for someone with years of experience in a particular industry or industries. If you are a brand new job seeker with limited experience perhaps consider adding more 'soft skills' you have developed such as teamwork, dedication and commitment; and highlight activities that show how you can make an important contribution such as volunteer work, fundraising or membership in community or other groups. Even if you have never worked before you might be surprised by how much 'Work' experience you can add to your résumé.

Challenging will be taking a 10, 15- or 20-year work history and condensing all relevant points into two pages. If you have a lot of information to include, I would suggest detailing the last 10-15 years. Of course, this will be much easier if you have held just one or two jobs over that time frame. If you do feel that you have way too much information to include because of a lengthier work history, consider the following tips.

- Only list relevant information. Meaning - add only past places of employment that are relevant to the job you are applying to.

- Create a more functional résumé that lists overall skills and successes while bullet pointing where you have worked.

- Go back 10-15 years and add a line saying something like; *"Details on prior employment available upon request."*

If you have held just one job concentrate on the value, you brought to your current or recent place of employment. Did you increase sales? Reduce turnover? Accomplish specific projects?

Remember - a recruiter might not fully understand the type of work you have done but they will understand Success! Highlighting successes, you have had and wins you brought for your employer will show what you might be able to bring to the company you are applying to.

Remembering that a recruiter might not understand the work or jobs you have done in the past is actually quite important. I have seen résumés where for example the candidates, coming from a very technical position were applying for other roles in a vastly different industries yet presented their experience using very technical jargon and insider terminology. A more general recruiter or even a specialist recruiter in the target industry would most likely have no idea what was being spoken about. Remember the audience and don't confuse them or overwhelm them with overly technical descriptions. They will potentially lose interest and not see the value that lies behind the descriptions!

To read more about the ideal length of your résumé read: https://www.businessinsider.com/résumé-length-two-pages-or-one-2018-11

Your Personal Details.

Your personal section is critical. After all, you want people to be able to contact you. I can't express the importance however of making sure that you review this section and make sure that your contact details are accurate and up to date. You would not believe how many applications and résumés I receive where the phone number is no longer in service or the applicant tells me that they moved some time ago, so the address is not current.

Be sure to provide an email address too and please…please - make sure you have an email address with a professional ring to it. Yourname@…… will suffice. Please avoid email names that might raise eyebrows or worse; cause alarm! One fellow I received an application from had an email address that suggested he really liked guns! While he may be a competitive target shooter (he wasn't actually) a handle like that would immediately distract from what may have otherwise been a great application! The small things really do count.

If you have a LinkedIn account (more on that later) be sure to provide the address here too. Some job seekers have a personal website too or a 'professional' Facebook page where they show off examples of their work (great if you are in photography, graphic arts, renovations or similar fields - an online portfolio if you will...) Add the address of these and other Social Media sites too in the Personal Details section; but only if they are relevant to your job search. I'd avoid adding personal Facebook, Snap Chat or Tik Tok account details!

Where are you located?

Having worked all over the world and interviewed thousands of people from all corners of the globe I have seen almost every type of résumé you can think of. One thing that became clear early on for me was how different parts of the world have different expectations when it comes to what information should and shouldn't be included.

Many European, African and Asian countries tend to 'allow' or accept that it is customary to include very personal details on a résumé. It will not be uncommon for me to see a résumé from India or France that includes a photo of the applicant, age or date of birth and even marital status! In some locations, adding information about marital status, number of children, nationality and date of birth is even required.

For a North American or British recruiter or hiring manager with perhaps little experience in recruiting people from overseas, seeing a photo or the candidate's marital status or religion on a résumé will almost cause a shock! In Canada, such details are never included on a résumé, whereas in Poland - it is expected that a professional headshot photo will be included.

Canada, the UK and the United States have very strict rules and standards when it comes to employment, interviewing and considering applicants. Never for example is a company to consider how many children a candidate has, whether he or she is married or how old they are. Disqualifying a candidate for these reasons violates numerous Human Rights laws across Canada and other similar equity laws in various countries. Companies therefore tend to not want to know these details about applicants (in fact, adding them may result in your application being disqualified) so that they can maintain as transparent and fair hiring process as possible that concentrates only on the candidate's skills, expertise, professional and academic backgrounds. For this reason, you are not required to include photos, your age or very personal details that are not relevant to the job. If you are unsure do a quick Google search to find out the best approach to take.

Employment Experience

In the 'Employment' or 'Work History' section you will provide the names of the companies you worked for, when you worked for them and what your position was. This is the basic amount of information you need to provide. To stand out however, go beyond what is referred to here as a laundry list. Add one or two key points about not only what you did but specifically any accomplishments you are proud of. What did you do in those jobs that benefitted the company? What successes did you have? If for example you had a Sales job and made several thousands or millions in sales, put that down. That's something that a hiring manager will want to see.

Don't go too crazy writing every accomplishment you had or everything you did that makes you proud or gave you satisfaction. Remember, this is a Résumé; a quick snapshot about who you are.

Again, lacking any hard and fast rules about how much information you should add - err on the side of keeping is concise. State what you did and what you accomplished in no more than 4-5 points. Listing everything you did in a job will not impress the reader and may actually make them give up on your résumé. You want to keep the reader engaged, focused and interested in what you have to say.

List the last 5 - 10 or so years of jobs. If you have had one job in that time and want to add earlier employment - go ahead. Or, you may have had only one job. This is fine. Everyone starts somewhere and hiring managers know this. Listing only one job however will give you more space in your résumé to add more information about successes, wins and accomplishments.

If adding more than on position to your résumé, be sure to start with the most recent, or the job you are currently at; and work backwards chronologically.

USE KEYWORDS!

Many of you will have had experience will online job boards or sending your résumés by email to a specific email address at the company that is hiring. What happens to this email? Sometimes it lands  in someone's inbox directly but in many cases, it feeds directly into a database created just for that job within a larger system called an Applicant Tracking System.

When the recruiter or hiring manager wants to review the people that have applied they can either do it manually by opening each résumé or they can set parameters in the system that 'parses' or screens the résumés received based upon specific variables based on key words. If you are applying for a Sales job, the system might 'screen-in' résumés that contain words such as Sales, Account Management, Cold Calling etc etc.

So, what can you do to help ensure your résumé makes it through this 'parsing' process? What key words can you use to make sure your résumé gets read? While giving an honest account of your experience, look at the language in the Job advertisement and incorporate that language or terms and expressions into your Work experience section where appropriate.

If the company is looking for a Sales Executive with Pharmaceutical Experience and a knowledge of CRM platforms such as Salesforce then not using the terms; Sales, Executive, Pharmaceutical, Salesforce may exclude your résumé from further consideration. At the very least, including those terms will capture the eye of the recruiter.

Some online job boards do not allow you to upload a résumé and instead ask you to complete a number of fields on the job application page. The same rules will apply with the use of keywords perhaps more so. Instances like this a rarer however than jobs opportunities that ask you to upload or email a prepared résumé.

Should you upload a résumé to a job board or after following the steps after clicking 'Apply,' ensure you upload a Word version of your résumé and not a PDF. Most ATS platforms are very text based and have a hard time reading through PDF files.

Okay - we've covered the basics of the Work Experience section. Now it's time for you to show how smart you are and list your educational accomplishments. Just a final note....Be careful to not flood your résumé with keywords - this too will stand out and may count against you. I have also heard of some people preparing résumés and including tons of key words in the blank areas of their résumé and changing the colour of the text to white so that they remain hidden. I highly, highly recommend against doing this.

Education

Much like the Work Experience section; you will list, in chronological order, working backwards; your Education.

How far back should you go? This too depends on how far you have gone! Let's say you have a PhD. Would you list where you went to High School? Perhaps not. You will most definitely name the school you obtained your Doctorate at and where you completed Graduate and Undergraduate studies.

Some suggest that if you went so far as a Bachelor or Associates degree you would provide the name of the university you completed your degree at and then provide where you completed College or High School. Personally, I would not add High School. That you have a degree tends to suggest that you completed secondary school level education.

In short, a rule of thumb is to go back 2-3 levels to no further back than High School. I have seen résumés as part of a candidate's application that included the name of the primary school they attended. One person even provided the name of the Kindergarten nursery they went to!!! This is definitely not required under any circumstances!

When providing your listing of educational establishments attended, provide the years of attendance, name of school and the level you attained. Always be sure to provide a factual record of educational achievements. It is not uncommon for a potential employer to ask for copies of certificates issued or confirmation that you did receive for example a Bachelor level degree. If you attended University but did not complete the course of study leading to the award of a degree, simply indicate the years you attended.

Definitely add all relevant certificates or courses you have completed; especially if they are relevant to the job you are interested in. List these after 'formal' education even if they were completed more recently. If you have fewer 'formal' education details to list, then for sure - highlight your certificates and completed courses.

Grade Point Average

Should you list your GPA if you are at University? I am a little on the fence about this. Definitely mentioned if your graduated with Honors/Honours or Summa Cum Laude for example but honestly - I have never heard a recruiter state "Wow - this guy has a 3.5 GPA!!!!"

I have however seen job postings that as a requirement mention applicants must have a certain GPA and above. In these cases, definitely mention it. If uncertain, I would leave it off.

Keep it Current

There is a truism in the world of academia that one needs to publish or perish. Graduate and specifically postgraduate students are expected to get their name out there and not only tell the world that they are subject matter experts but add to the general body of knowledge they are concerned with. This is accomplished through contributing to journals and periodicals and either teaching or speaking engagements.

What does this have to do with job hunting? Are there any lessons we can take from this? Most definitely. It's all about keeping ourselves current and our skill sets and experience relevant to the job market today. A lot of us have been in the same position for the same employer for a number of years. We may have taken a lot of in-house, job-specific courses, but how much of that training is transferable to other employers? We all know people who were laid off or down sized after a lengthy career with one employer (you may have even been the victim of this) and suddenly forced into a position where they had to write résumés and start a job search after being out of the 'game' for a number of years. I recently did some pro bono coaching for a lady who had just lost her husband who was the major family breadwinner. At 65 she had to now look at getting into the workforce. She had no résumé and her most recent job was almost 20 years ago. Not the strongest of positions to be in.

Hiring managers will look at résumés and in the back of their mind keep asking themselves if there is anything in them that is relevant to the job they are hiring for even if they offer full training to learn the basics of the position. Relevancy does not necessarily mean related skills and experience but can point to an ability to learn and take on new challenges. It is easy to become somewhat complacent in a secure job that offers a steady and reliable pay cheque. We are all guilty of this. The worst position to then find oneself in is having to scramble and upgrade and become ready for change when change suddenly hits us one Monday morning - much like the lady mentioned above.

How can we keep it current and show we can take on new challenges? Stay involved and keep up-grading skills. Be honest about skills and experiences you have and whether or not they would be transferable to another field or employer? Technology and business processes are changing with increasing rapidity. Our five, ten and or 20-year-old résumés are expected to compete in this landscape.

There is an abundance of courses and training programs, available both on-line and in person, we can look at taking.

Many of these are free and a large number of them are offered within your own community at various government funded agencies. There are a number of associations we can look at joining too. I mentioned LinkedIn above. LinkedIn offers dozens of associations and groups you can join and participate in. Such involvement can definitely be included in a résumé.

If you haven't come across it (I am not affiliated with them in any way); udemy.com is a site that offers thousands of training courses - some as low as $15, which can be completed in a day. The quality  of the courses is fantastic, and they provide you with an opportunity to not only stay current but to keep adding to your résumé. An amazing option if you've been out of school for some time and need to quickly get up to speed with a new skillset.

Not only can we keep current by taking training; joining groups and associations allows us to constantly refresh our résumés and ourselves as candidates. If we look at our résumé as a weapon in the fight for a job we really want, we need to be better armed than our opponents; i.e. other candidates.

Think of your résumé as a work in progress; something you are constantly polishing and upgrading. Don't let it gather dust. Not only are you investing in yourself, but you are nurturing the one thing that will get your foot in the door.

Honesty is the Best Policy

It is widely believed that candidates will try to show their very best on a résumé. Why wouldn't they - they want the job they are applying for after all!! The temptation may be to over inflate experience, responsibilities or length of service. Always err on the side of caution. If you perhaps filled in for a supervisor every now and then, should you put 'Supervisor' as a title you held? I would suggest not. However, I would try to add that you were called upon to perform supervisory duties.

If you perhaps attended the first year of a university program and then left to pursue other activities would you say you have a Bachelor degree? Again; I would suggest not but I have seen candidates say they have a degree when in fact they did not even graduate!!

Even worse perhaps is to add details or experience you do not actually even have!

Recently I was interviewing a hopeful job seeker who had just arrived in Canada. He told me that he had only been here for a few weeks. While reviewing his résumé with him however I noticed that he had listed having worked at a company in Toronto. I asked him about this and enquired as to why he left a job he landed so quickly after having just arrived? His response shocked me (and after having seen thousands of résumés and interviewed hundreds of people it is hard to shock me). He said he didn't actually work there and has never in fact worked in Canada! I asked him why he would add something that wasn't true? He responded by saying that his friend told him to add it as it looks better if you add some recent work experience!!!!

I assured him that this was not the case and in fact will make the interviewer question your integrity.

Unfortunately, this job seeker was totally unprepared for the job search process in Canada and he was given some (well-meaning perhaps) terribly bad advice. I gave him the benefit of the doubt to help him find a job which he was in sore need of. A lot of employers I have spoken to when faced with similar situations have refused to proceed any further with candidates questioning their integrity and eventually dependability as employees.

If a company is interested in you and call you in for an interview they will spend some time doing research on where you worked and went to school and if you make it to the interview they will most likely ask you very specific questions. The reason for this is two-fold: To learn a little more about you and your experience and capabilities and to confirm everything you listed on your résumé.

You can be certain too that the company will conduct reference checks (see below) on you as well to get confirmation about who you are as an employee, how you worked and if everything you listed is accurate.

With résumés and job applications, like anything in life, honesty is the best policy. Do not over exaggerate experience or qualifications. The recruiter or hiring manager will soon uncover inconsistencies or inaccuracies. Many in fact may employ a reference checking service who will dig further into your background. Honesty, Honesty, Honesty is the best policy.

There have been cases where people were discovered after having started work that there were misleading details in their application, and they were eventually terminated.

Companies not only focus on success but sustainability and risk mitigation. The concern is about the reliability of the people on the team. If this is ever in question, they will not think twice about parting ways with you.

Explaining Gaps in your Résumé.

Many hiring manager and recruiters often notice very quickly gaps in your employment history. The belief here; perhaps misguided, is that there must be something amiss if you have long gaps between jobs. If you do have gaps in your employment history be ready to explain why. My own team of recruiters often ask people what they were doing between jobs for it is how they answer that often details the type of employee that are or might be.

For example I recently heard my senior recruiter interviewing a candidate as to why he left his last job and what he has been doing in the almost year and a half since he had worked. He replied - "Not much really - helped out around the house" ! What?? In 18 months this candidate had not been able to find work in his field, during a period of unprecedented growth and a labour shortage in his region; and ostensibly had done little more than hang around the house!

If he had answered, "I decided to dedicate some time on personal development and cultivating soft career skills to help propel me to the next level,' or; "I decided to take a number of upgrading courses and work on establishing a small side business..." we would have looked at him in a very different light indeed.

There is a belief that extensive pauses between jobs needs to be explained for the immediate conclusion is that the candidate may have sat at home doing nothing.

Other reasons such as maternity or paternity leave or taking care of a sick relative will be readily understood however and you should not be placed in a position where you will have to give any further explanation.

TIP: Be ready to explain absences from the work force when interviewing with a hiring manager or recruiter. It may be worthwhile to indicate on your résumé the reasons for a gap in employment.

References

It is very common - indeed it is a standard part of the job process that you will be asked to provide the names and contact details of Referees at previous places of employment who can attest to your having worked at that company and to confirm the work you did and how you performed as a member of the team.

References are designed to not only find out what kind of employee you are but are part of wider risk management. They want to know if there is anything in your background at previous places of employment that might cause an issue later on.

Generally, companies will ask you for the names and numbers of two - perhaps three people they can speak to at previous places of employment and in many cases, the decision to offer you a job will be dependent upon successful reference checking having been completed.

A few rules of thumb to follow.

If you have not already informed a current employer that you intend to leave and have started interviewing elsewhere; do not give them as references. It might be embarrassing for all involved if you are still working and nobody knows you intend to resign.

Make sure everyone who you are providing as references is aware. It is good to ask their permission first if they are okay to provide prospective employers with an employment reference for you.

Ensure that you are giving someone you reported to as a reference. Companies will generally not accept co-workers, family or friends as references.

How in depth the reference call will be depends on the level of job you are applying for. If you are applying for a more entry level position this call may only take a couple of minutes and will be simply to confirm your dates of employment, how you performed and why you left. In most cases the person making the call will ask your referee if they would hire you again (hypothetically) should a similar position become available. We hope that the answer will be Yes!!

Past employers will tend to not want to say anything negative and if they feel they cannot give you a positive reference will advise the caller that they have 'No Response,' or something to that effect.

Be prepared with references and ensure that you are giving the names of people who can actually be reached. Companies may offer you a position *dependent* on them obtaining references on you. Hard to reach people might slow down your chances of getting a job!

Should you list the names and contact details of referees (the formal name for one who you are listing to provide a reference) on your résumé? Some do but I tend to suggest not to.

If a company is very interested in you, they will ask for the names of people they can contact. This will show that you are in serious consideration and a good way to track how your application is faring.

So you've sent in a fantastic résumé. It passed the ATS program and was shortlisted for further review by a recruiter.

Make your Résumé easy to read.

Regardless of the job you are applying for; the sophistication of the ATS they are using - at some point a human reader will hold your résumé in their hands. Don't think they will spend hours reviewing it. With most jobs accepting applications online more and more people are applying for a job which means dozens of résumés for a recruiter to read through - in some cases lot more - depending on the job. Believe it or not - your résumé may only be given a 12-15 second review before the recruiter decides what the next step should be.

Keep your résumé user friendly - make it easy to read and also predictable. You would be surprised if I were to tell you how many 5-6 page résumés I received with size 9 font and jam packed with details. This does not help your chances.

If anything, it will tell a potential employer that you do not know how to be concise and make a targeted and rational argument!!

If you are reading this, chances you started at the top of the page and read left to right. Résumés are read in the same way too. Lay out your information in an easy to follow format: (starting from the top) Name. Address. Phone. Email. Work Experience. Education. Technical Skills...... A recruiter's eye is almost trained to scan through résumés very quickly seeking out specific information. Make sure they can find it. Don't include lengthy paragraphs, long lists and most of all keep it simple. There are lots of very fancy résumé formats out there with information spread all over the page, in side bars, in little boxes; often with little icons. Honestly - recruiters do not like this. Yes - your résumé may look fancy, but fancy is not the objective here. Getting a job is. Don't make it hard for a recruiter to find the information they are looking for. If they have to work too hard they will put your résumé in 'that' pile - where you don't want it to end up!

If you are starting a résumé from scratch - consider a layout such as the one on the next page. Might not look fancy but works with most ATS systems and is nice and clear for the recruiter to read!

John Parsons

NAME NAME

email @email.com City, State/Province (555) 555-5555

EXECUTIVE SUMMARY
A couple of lines explaining who you are and the value your bring

KEY SKILLS
Sales | Team Leadership | Other skills relevant to the job

RECENT EXPERIENCE

EMPLOYER NAME
City, State | Job Title | Dates

Key Responsibilities
- Responsibility/Achievements
- Responsibility/Achievements
- Responsibility/Achievements

EMPLOYER NAME
City, State | Job Title | Dates

Key Responsibilities
- Responsibility/Achievements
- Responsibility/Achievements
- Responsibility/Achievements

EDUCATION

Degree Title (Year Awarded)
School Name | City, State

Degree Title (Year Awarded)
School Name | City, State

- Additional Certification (if any) | Issuing Organization | Year
- Additional Certification (if any) | Issuing Organization | Year
- Additional Certification (if any) | Issuing Organization | Year

TECHNICAL SKILLS

List Software Hardware Skills. eg MS Office | SQL | Java | SalesForce | Oracle

VOLUNTEER WORK

**Mention any volunteer activities you are currently involved in.
Companies like hearing about this.**

As you can see, each section is clearly identified, it is clear and there is plenty of white space on the page.

Winning the Job Hunt

Avoid using Icons.

Notice too that there are no little icons or pictures such as those above indicating e-mail addresses or phone numbers. They really have no place in a professional résumé and look a little comic book like. Importantly however, a lot of ATS systems get tripped up by them and may make a lot of your content unreadable!

Avoid putting your content in tables – I see this a lot – especially when receiving résumés directly by email. ATS systems often do not read what is inside tables. Imaging spending hours creating a résumé only to have an ATS platform think you sent in a blank document!!!!! Plain text – all the way.....

Shall I send a Cover Letter?

A lot of mixed opinions out there about this one. Whether or not to include one is a decision often made by the application system itself – especially online systems that ask you to upload just your résumé.

You will come across job ads that do ask you to submit a cover letter and a résumé. They don't want to just hear about what you have done (in your résumé) but want to see a Cover Letter to see how you write and present yourself.

The rules of the résumé apply to the cover letter too. Be as concise and as on target as possible. Think of the cover letter as an introduction to your résumé and application. Do not – like some do – repeat the entire résumé in it. Use it as an opportunity to express the awesome things you will do for the company. Keeping your cover letter to just a few short paragraphs; explain;

- How you are excited about the opportunity to apply.
- The value you will bring.
- What amazing things you will do in the role.
- How you look forward to hearing from them.

That's it. Nice and simple. Avoid, in your cover letter and your résumé, explaining that you are applying because this is an opportunity that will help you grow and will help with your career development. A potential employer does not want to hear how his or her investment in you will be paid off by you leaving because you have learned great skills and are now ready to apply them elsewhere.

Again, be sparse with the details, your letter will be skimmed through. Do not beat the reader down with like one candidate recently who did send a three-page, single spaced cover letter typed in size 9 Times New Roman. It was a little painful to get through and I gave up.

If you see an ad where you are asked to e-mail your résumé directly to a person, you can attach your cover letter too but at the very least; always add a couple of prefacing lines in the email body. Avoid, as is becoming increasingly common; attaching your résumé to an empty email with just the word 'Job' in the subject line. The candidate who stands out will be the one who crafts a few well written lines accompanying their résumé

John Parsons

The Phone Interview

Out of the blue; most likely when you least expect it - your phone will ring and someone at the other end of the line will say "Hi - can I speak to …….. please; this is Ms Smith from ABC Company. I'm calling about your application…"

Firstly - congratulations. You will notice many job postings saying something along the lines of …'only qualified candidates will be contacted.' So, if you've received a call this is a great step. It means that your résumé has made it through the initial screening and the recruiter or hiring manager wants to talk to you a little more. This is no small accomplishment. Reports suggest that only 3 to 5% of applicants will receive a call back. This is where it truly gets real.

Winning the Job Hunt

You'll never know when you might get a call. It might be minutes after sending your résumé or it could be days or even weeks later. Always be prepared for a call from a recruiter. This means that you want to sound energetic, interested and engaged in the conversation.

Speak to the caller as if you know exactly why they are calling. Now this might sound strange. Some job seekers will send out several, if not dozens of résumés. That's great if you are looking for a job but bear in mind the recruiter is calling you about ONE job at their company. Do not - and I repeat - do not - never say "Who is this and what job is it for? I sent so many résumés out…" Act and sound like you know why exactly she is calling and where she is calling from. I've heard this and honestly - it kills it for the employer. It tells me nothing more than there was no real thought about applying to the job.

On that note - ONLY apply for jobs after really considering what it is; where it is and the hours of work. ONLY apply if you want THAT job. I called a candidate not too long ago to phone screen him and after describing the position (basically repeating the job ad) he replied; '*No - it's not really what I'm looking for...*" What? You made me spend the time reading; and re-reading your résumé, shortlisting you and then calling for you to tell me that you are not interested? Then why apply? Not the best feeling to leave a recruiter with should you one day wish to apply for another position with that company - and it does happen.

Keep a handy list of all the companies you have applied to if you have sent out multiple applications. List the name of the company; where they are located; what service product line they are involved in and when you applied....

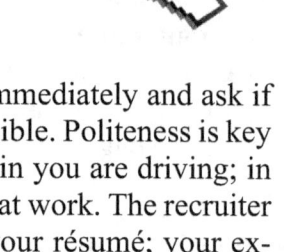

If you cannot talk - tell them so immediately and ask if you can return their call as soon as possible. Politeness is key here. Don't just say I can't talk. Explain you are driving; in a loud public place or maybe currently at work. The recruiter wants to have a chat with you about your résumé; your experience and the job you are applying for. Ensure that not only are you free to talk but you are in a location conducive to a private phone conversation. They will appreciate this.

The Interview

CONGRATULATIONS!! YOU'VE LANDED AN INTERVIEW!!!!!!!

Believe it or not; being called in for an interview is a significant step. You've almost made it to the end!

Making it through to the interview stage is a great sign. The recruiter might have sifted through dozens of résumés, shortlisted potential candidates and already conducted dozens of phone screen interviews.

Formal interviews are still very standard steps to go through for most jobs and are a very important, if not the most important part of the process although in a lot of companies these are becoming more and more informal. Always be prepared however for a formal meeting with a prospective employer. Indeed, be prepared to face a panel interview depending on the level of job you are applying for where more than one representative of the company will be sitting across the table from you.

Most likely the interview will start with a few pleasantries - asking you if you found the location without any trouble, a few comments about the weather etc - pretty much those things you might chat briefly about with someone you get into an elevator with.

Of course, you will be asked to sit. Unless the interviewer is already sitting, I would suggest waiting for the interviewer to take her or his seat before you take yours. It might be customary to be offered coffee or a water. I always suggest not to take one and politely say no; saying you had one just prior to the interview. First, I doubt many interviewers actually expect anyone to say yes and from what I have heard it leaves many interviewees feeling uncomfortable. When do they take a sip? What if they spill something; Where do they put their cup once they have finished? Be on the safe side and politely decline. Again, in most cases it is almost just a rhetorical question as opposed to a genuine offer to provide you with a beverage!

While the interviewer will have reviewed your résumé and will most likely have one in front of them or perhaps on the screen of their computer it is always a great idea to carry a couple of copies with you. For this purpose, it is recommended that you carry a small folder or presentation binder with you with additional copies. Perhaps the interviewer doesn't have one handy in which case you can offer a fresh copy. It is also great to have to review and scan when asking questions about your experience. It also looks good to walk into the interview with a binder or folder - it lends an air of professionalism and that you are taking the process seriously.

The interviewer already has a sense they like you as a candidate and use the interview as a step to get to know you better - to drill down into your experience and previous work history.

Questions you can anticipate during the interview will be similar to:

- What interests you about this job? this company?
- Why are you looking at leaving your current employer?
- What have you been doing since your last job?
- What do you know about this company?
- Tell me a little more about what you are doing now,
- What are your salary expectations?

With regards to salary expectations I am still unsure why many interviewers ask this question. They already know how much they are going to offer you; the pay rate may have been in the job ad. If anything, it is to validate that what they are offering is in line with what you are hoping to get and not necessarily a question to see if they need to offer you more. If they do, then fantastic but I doubt this will happen.

Doing a little research in order to answer the above questions will show that you are engaged, interested in what they have to offer.

Behavioural Descriptive Interviews

An interviewer will have a good understanding of what you have done and your accomplishments from your résumé but in certain cases they may want to dig a little deeper and find out more about you and specifically; how you will act in certain situations. They will ask you questions based on hypothetical situations. An example might be:

"Let's say you have a customer and they are incredibly unhappy with the product or service they received. How would you handle this?" Or;

"Tell me about a time when you went above and beyond to provide amazing customer service."

These are both BDI type of interview questions. For sure you will feel like you've been put on the spot and in a way, this is what the interviewer wants to do.

First thing - don't rush to answer - take a breath and a pause. Then follow the STAR method. You have been asked to respond to a question about situation in your professional past. Break down your thought process and your response in the following way.

Situation: Explain briefly what happened. What did the customer say? What was the issue?

Task: What was your job at the time? What were you responsible for?

Action: What did you do to try to resolve the issue? Was it successful?

Result: How did things end? Was everyone happy? Did you save the sale and avoid lost business?

Of course, it is difficult to plan for every situation but think of a number of events where there was a potential problem and you resolved it and frame it is using the STAR method.

According to indeed.com's Career Guide, the most common type questions you might run into are:

1. Tell me about a time when you handled a challenging situation.

2. Tell me about a time when you made a mistake.

3. Tell me about a time when you were in conflict with a colleague.

4. Tell me about how you work under pressure.

5. Give me an example of how you set goals.

6. Have you ever made an unpopular decision?

7. Tell me about a goal you set and how you achieved it.

8. Tell me about a goal you failed to achieve.

9. Tell me about a time you disagreed with a supervisor.

10. Tell me about a time you had to stand up for your beliefs.

11. Can you share about a time you had to be flexible or adaptable?

12. Talk about a time when you've had to manage up.

13. Tell me about a time when you felt like a good leader.

14. Tell me about your proudest moment in your professional career.

15. Tell me about a time you had to learn quickly.

16. Tell me about a time when you had to say "no."

17. Give me an example of a time you had to prioritize certain tasks.

18. Tell me about a time you made a difficult decision.

19. Tell me about the best presentation you've given. Was it good?

20. Tell me about a time when you disagreed with your manager.

21. Tell me about a time when you had to solve a problem.

22. Was there a time when you felt dissatisfied with your work?

23. Tell me about a time you felt you went above and beyond.

24. Have you ever made huge impact at a previous company?

www.indeed.com/career-advice/interviewing/most-common-behavioral-interview-questions-and-answers

Dress For Success and To Impress

I remember a candidate who came in for an interview wearing no shoes. It's true. He rollerbladed to my office, took his skates off in the waiting area and walked into the interview room in his jeans and t-shirt with just socks on his feet. Needless to say, the interview took about 5 seconds and he was not offered a position.

Choosing what to wear for an interview is perhaps one of the easiest parts of the job seeking process yet sadly one very often overlooked. We tend to formulate opinions about people within the first few seconds of meeting them. Nowhere is this truer than in the job interview.

A lot of people tend to think that because they are applying for an entry level position or a more physical, manual type job that they do not really need to dress to impress. Although the work attire for the job a manager is recruiting for may include coveralls, jeans or sweatshirts we shouldn't make the mistake in believing that attending an interview dressed in this manner conveys we are right for the job. It may be true but unfortunately gives the idea that we don't really care about making a good impression and just threw anything on before showing up.

I'm not advocating a three-piece suit for every interview, but we can never go wrong with business – casual in the absence of knowing what is acceptable in whatever company you are interviewing at – even if the position is entry-level. Of course, an interview for a senior position might require more formal business attire. Jeans, t-shirts and sneakers, however, should always be avoided.

Many interviews take place in small meeting rooms behind closed doors. It's best to keep perfumes and colognes to a minimum if worn at all (some workplaces even ask employees to refrain from wearing them). Smokers should pay attention to the lingering smell of cigarette smoke on the breath and on clothing. It is best maybe to avoid smoking completely before an interview as mints or chewing gum really do not mask the smell that well! On that note - I once met an applicant; clearly a heavy smoker, who dropped off his résumé that must have been sitting on a desk in a small room with no windows in which he chain smoked. The résumé reeked of cigarettes! We had to copy it (we are required to keep résumés for a year) and destroy the original.

How you dress for an interview is an unspoken signal about how important the interview is to you and how you want to be perceived. It tells the interviewer whether or not you really want the job. If you are unsure about what to wear, as mentioned above, you can always rely on business-casual at a bare minimum and take it up a notch or two depending on the seniority of the position. If you are interviewing for a corporate, office position you can always visit a day or so ahead and look at what current employees are wearing. This will tell you something about the organization's culture and specifically its dress code.

You're building on the success of your application, résumé and phone interview. You've done well getting to the in-person interview. Dress to impress and show them you want and deserve the job!

John Parsons

Let me get Honest and Real with you…. The Untold Truth About Interviews…

Hiring managers and recruiters can be harsh…. maybe not to your face directly but some will pick up on the smallest details and that is all they will focus on. They'll look at you immediately and question whether or not you are a good fit for the organization often before they drill down and get to know you and discuss your qualifications! In most cases, they know if you have the job before you've even taken a seat!

The interview is in many cases, simply a chance to put a face to a name and to double check a few details.

But interviewers can be a picky bunch and let a lot of pre-conceived ideas and thoughts get in the way.

Should hiring managers stick to the objective facts about you and the requirements of the job? Ideally; Yes. But in reality, they let personal opinions, likes and dislikes get in the way. One hiring manager I know refuses - absolutely refuses to look at a candidate's qualifications or ability to do the job if he senses the candidate is a smoker. Not because there is a company policy against hiring smokers - he just dislikes the habit so much that he can't see beyond that.

It is so true that people - especially interviewers, will develop a lasting impression about you within seconds of meeting you. Don't give them anything to react against. Be professionally deferential, polite and don't forget to smile!!

Dealing With Why You Left Your Last Job

Everyone has a history. We've all worked in places we didn't like. We've had bosses and co-workers we didn't like being around. Be honest - how many times have you thought your supervisor, manager or boss was not fit to do the job and you thought you could do it yourself?

Often an interviewer will ask why you left your last or another job? Don't tell them what someone recently told me... *"I quit because the guy didn't know how to run the company and he was useless when it came to dealing with clients."* What???? Firstly, you have no idea what the owner was going through on a daily basis and why wouldn't you step up to help if you thought he was struggling?

If you have ever had issues with a previous company or employer - under no circumstances reveal this in an interview. Before you say *'Who would do that..."* like the fellow above, it happens way too often.

A recruiter hearing information like that will immediately think – *"If they are saying that about a previous employer without really knowing me, what will they end up saying about us?" "What kind of attitude will they have at work?"* Chances are if you start complaining about a previous place of employment you might as well pick up your belongings and leave the interview.

Rather than discussing all the negatives about a previous employer; put a positive spin on why you left or justify it in a way that makes sense.

"A new company took over and there was an internal reorganization and I was downsized."

"I decided to take some time away and work on upgrading my skills."

"I had to look for something closer to home."

Make sure though that there is an element of truth to your answer because they may ask you to explain further.

Social Media and the Job Hunt

When it comes to Social Media, we immediately think of more entertainment focused sites like Facebook and Pinterest. What a lot of job hunters don't know is how relevant various Social Media platforms can be in the employment hunting process. Indeed, a well-rounded job search needs to incorporate a concerted and dedicated social media strategy.

Using LinkedIn.

First - why should you use LinkedIn (linkedin.com)? Well - it is where people go online to network and importantly; where recruiters go to find candidates for jobs! It is estimated that approximately 95% of recruiters in North America use LinkedIn to source candidates. That's a lot of people potentially searching for you to offer you a job!! Additional reports also suggest that LinkedIn has over 675 monthly users; 40% of which use it every day! Adding to this that "61 million users

are considered senior level influencer and 40 million are in decision-making positions," make it a great platform to consider getting on to.
(source: https://foundationinc.co/lab/b2b-marketing-linkedin-stats/)

It's not just the decision makers however that are the driving force behind why LinkedIn is useful. Of the 675 million users mentioned above a huge number of them in your industry will be great contacts and leads; people you can network with; learn things from and share information with. Who knows how many of them will prove to be great leads in the future?

So, What Is LinkedIn and How Do I Use It?

Think Facebook for business. Perhaps the easiest way to describe LinkedIn is as an online résumé with a built-in capability allowing users to join industry and interest specific groups. Members can then post messages to other group followers and receive regular summaries of recent posts. Where hard or soft copy résumés are suggested to be no longer than 2 to 3 pages, you can fill your LinkedIn profile with a plethora of added details about past experience and education, interests and even books you are reading. Colleagues, business associates or clients can even add recommendations to your profile.

If you are used to using Facebook, you will get LinkedIn. You build your Connections (Friends) by sending Connection requests. LinkedIn will also make suggestions of who you might want to connect with based on what you do, where you you have worked and where you went to school.

Recruiters have long seen the value of LinkedIn as a search tool and I doubt that many candidate searches begin without looking at LinkedIn as a primary step. Joining LinkedIn is free and while there is an option to pay a monthly fee for expanded access to various services, the basic membership can serve you well. Once you have joined and created your profile, be sure to add your LinkedIn address to the contact details section of your hard and soft copy résumé.

This morning I received my weekly update from 'Ex Canadian Forces,' one of the LinkedIn groups I'm a member of. Another member posted a message yesterday indicating that he just retired from the Forces as a Logistics Officer and is seeking civilian employment in the same field in or near the Ottawa region. I immediately contacted him, asked for his résumé and told him a colleague in Ottawa is frequently looking for Logistics and Distribution professionals for clients she works for. Within minutes we were communicating via email and shortly thereafter I forwarded his résumé on for him. We'll have to see what happens but very quickly, through the networking capabilities of LinkedIn, his résumé was in the hands of a recruitment specialist working within the industry and city he is interested in.

Promoting Yourself on LinkedIn

LinkedIn is amazing as a static online résumé. But if nobody knows about your profile or search specifically for you, they may never see it or realize what a great candidate you are. Think of a website. Might be the best-looking website there is but without ongoing and effective Search Engine Optimization and fresh content - people may never see it! Same thing with LinkedIn. Now - many of the ways in which we can promote a website through SEO are not available to us on LinkedIn but there are definitely ways to stand out and get noticed. Primarily this will be through **Activity** and creating engaging content that gives value to others.

LinkedIn Activity

LinkedIn Activity can be any number of things just like it is on Facebook. You can scroll through your timeline, liking posts as you go; or you can comment and share. But if you want to use LinkedIn to start getting known and making contacts you might want to consider creating your own content. This doesn't have to be complicated - or it can be as extensive as you want. Have something to say? Post it to LinkedIn. Want to share a great picture you came across? Post that to LinkedIn too. Make sure however that whatever you post is Business or Industry related. If not, you may incur the wrath of the LinkedIn purists who believe that the platform should only ever be about business related content.

Creating content is great. Getting people to engage with it is even better. The more people engage with your posts (liking, commenting and sharing) the higher you will score on the elusive LinkedIn Algorithm. Now this is a bit of mystery just like Facebook's and Instagram's algorithms, but it is believed that the higher you score on this - the more your content will be promoted to the timelines of others and ultimately; the more you will get known.

Once you post, drive engagement. Ask a question in your post. Ask people to comment or to leave their thoughts. Don't just post and move on. If anyone does comment or leave feedback - ALWAYS - comment back. Always like the comments left. Always like your own comments and responses to others' comments. All of this will tell the algorithm that your content is getting engagement. It takes a while but keep at it and stay consistent.

Hashtags!

Yep - they help drive LinkedIn too. In much the same way as Twitter or Instagram, hashtags make your posts more easily discoverable. When you post, think of relevant hashtags specific to your industry, location or business niche. Don't overdo it with hashtags - it looks spammy - and be sure to keep them professional!

A couple of LinkedIn Hashtag resources…

https://blog.hootsuite.com/linkedin-hastags-guide/

https://www.socialmediatoday.com/news/a-4-step-guide-to-using-hashtags-effectively-on-linkedin/568995/

LinkedIn Video Updates

Think of how you use Facebook. What type of posts interest you or make you stop to take a look? Chances are it is video. Video posts are easy to digest and much easier than reading lengthy text posts. For anyone just getting started on LinkedIn, video might be the fastest way to grow a large following and make a name for yourself. I know getting in front of a camera and broadcasting to potentially millions of people seems daunting but who cares?! People won't be watching your video to judge you - they will stop to listen to what you have to say and perhaps learn something. This is the key - the secret sauce.

People love value and getting value in easy to digest chunks. Very few people want to read lengthy books or articles anymore; but they will watch a video for sure. This is why YouTube has become so popular. No matter where you are in your career - getting started or a seasoned veteran - you have something to say that others will be interested in.

A new job seeker? Chronicle your job search adventure. Record a video before you go into an interview explaining how you prepared for it. Teach other job seekers what your strategy is. Are you an experienced Social Media Marketer? Why not record a *Getting Your Business on Social Media in 5 Steps* video? Or one on *How to Engage Your Audience and Win Customers on Instagram*?

All you need is a smart phone and the LinkedIn App. Don't record a video talking to thousands of viewers. Talk to just One person - the ideal person you think you will get something from what you are saying. Visual them and talk directly to them. It's not easy and takes practice but over time your videos will become better and better.

As I mentioned above - don't just post videos - add an intro comment first - use Hashtags. If you mention a resource or want to highlight certain points - add a comment to your own video (don't forget to Like your comment).

Here's a link that dives deeper into creating great LinkedIn video content…
https://biteable.com/blog/tips/linkedin-video/

LinkedIn Job Search

This has become incredibly awesome over the past few years and if you do nothing else on LinkedIn - use it for the

Job Search function it contains. You can drill down by job title and location. What is even better about it is that in most cases you can apply right from within the job listing and upload your résumé!

Depending on how complete your profile is, LinkedIn will tell you; based upon skills you list, if you are a match for the jobs that show up in the results. If you do pop up as being a match - apply for sure!

Twitter

It's hard to watch television today and not see a presenter's caption include a Twitter handle. Normally it is their name preceded by the @ sign. Most people tend to think, and with good reason, that Twitter.com is an online micro-blog allowing users to promote themselves in 280 characters or less or to tell the world where they are eating lunch! In many instances this is true. Recent experience however is showing that Twitter is fast becoming a popular job and candidate search resource. Recruiters are becoming increasingly proficient in searching for candidates within Twitter and will sift through Profiles and launch searches for various keywords relevant to the position they are hiring for. If you hashtag #Engineer in a tweet for example there is a possibility it will show up in the results of a recruiter's search for an #Engineer. Like LinkedIn, Twitter is completely free and affords you not only the opportunity to promote yourself, but it gives you the ability to follow a number of other users including corporate and agency recruiters posting openings they have.

Clearly job hunting today poses unique challenges and is not what it used to be. There is still a lot to be said for pounding the pavement and dropping résumés off but there is most definitely a shift occurring. Becoming familiar with how Social Media can enhance our job seeking efforts does take a little time but it is time well spent. Recruiters are spending more and more time in this 'space' and meeting them here can save you a lot of pavement time.

Here's another Link that explains how Twitter is great for Job Hunting.

https://www.jobscan.co/blog/how-to-use-twitter-in-your-job-search/

The Follow Up

A number of people have contacted me over the last little while about whether or not they should follow up with an employer once they have submitted a résumé in response to a job advertisement. In short – Yes!

There are a couple of tips that might help with your follow up and tell the hiring manager you are indeed serious about the job. There are also a couple of things you want to watch out for. Most definitely there is a 'way' to follow up.

A lot of job advertisements today state that only those being considered will be contacted for an interview. This is great for those who receive a call but what about those who don't? In some cases, it is difficult to get back to every single applicant; especially when the advertisement results in dozens if not hundreds of applicants. Getting back to candidates is something I strive to improve upon. Well-presented and well thought applications do receive a call-back even if it is to say, *'Thank you – we will consider you for the next opening'*. As I have mentioned before; hiring managers can recognize a targeted application and many will try to call the candidate either way.

If you are serious about a job and feel that you have submitted a 'competitive' application, then you will want to follow up. Again; this will show you are serious about getting the job and you may just prompt the hiring manager to take a look at your résumé again. If you haven't been successful, this will afford you the opportunity to ask why you didn't get the job. If it's a field you really want to get into you might want to ask what you are missing and what skill sets you can improve upon or what courses they recommend you take in order to be more successful next time. I know that the ultimate aim of an application is to get a job but not getting one can turn into a useful learning experience. Spending a few minutes on the phone with someone who regularly hires for that type of position is like speaking to a job coach or consultant for free. Take advantage of the time you get.

Give it a little time before following up. You can do this either by phone call or by email. I wouldn't recommend just showing up. The people you want to see might be occupied or attending to other matters and will not be able to give you the time needed to discuss your particular application. Email works fine and most hiring managers will respond to a question about your application. Waiting at least a week before following up is acceptable. If doing so by email, a simple *Dear Sir / Madam*; followed by a couple of lines stating who you are and that you are curious about the status of your application is fine.

I received an email recently that went something along the lines of: *"Are you people still hiring? I applied a couple of days ago and I didn't get a phone call."* Perhaps not the best way to approach a company as it might come across as a little unprofessional and pushy. How you apply for a job and how you follow up is an indication in the mind of the hiring manager how you might be as an employee.

Recently I received a call from a candidate who after introducing himself told me he had just sent an email in for the job and wanted more details. (First – he should have found out before he applied…) so we chatted for a few minutes. An hour later he called back to (rather passively aggressively), check the phone number we had for him. We did have the correct number.

Two hours later; another call to see if we had made a decision. This went beyond showing an interest. He was politely told we will be reviewing applications and getting back to him in due course. His repeated calls and demanding tone suggested nothing more than a lack of appreciation for our time and the process. He did end up receiving a call back saying he did not make it past the screening process. I can only imagine how he might behave on the job! (I told you I was going to give you some recruiter insights!!)

Always follow up. Think of yourself as a salesperson selling product You! Good salespeople always follow up with prospects once they have submitted a bid or proposal. It shows the potential customer that they want their business. Show you are interested and serious about getting the job. Be sure to allow the company a little time to review your application (please!!). Whether or not your application was successful, try to view the entire process as a learning experience and should you get to speak to the hiring manager, be sure to pick their brains clean! You'll never know what valuable insight you will get.

Wrapping It Up

So - there are a lot of points to consider. Much of what I have presented here is based on my thoughts, opinions and experience in the industry; recruiting thousands over the past number of years. Everyone has an opinion, and may not all agree with what I have written here. Some things are fairly agreed upon across the board, however. Sticking to a few key principles - you can't go wrong.

Make sure you send a well written, clear and targeted résumé. Some people say to not bother sending a cover letter as it doesn't get read. I disagree. Even if it is read through quickly; it shows you have taken to the time to really consider your application and you are very interested in this job.

Be prepared for the follow-up phone call. Show enthusiasm in your voice and let the caller believe that you have been waiting for their call with anticipation!

Business casual as a minimum for the interview. Never be late and carry a few copies of your résumé with you.

Prepare for the interview. Know what the company does; what the job entails and be prepared to answer BDI questions. Have a couple of questions of your own as for sure they will ask you at the end of the interview; "Do you have any questions?"

Wait a week and then follow up if you haven't heard anything.

Wait to receive the Job Offer and show through your awesomeness on the Job that they made the best hiring decision ever!

Congratulations on making it through to the end. If you need further help on preparing a résumé contact me through my résumé service available on Fiverr by heading over to www.fiverr.com/johnparsons01

For more information about custom career coaching and guidance connect with me on one of my social channels:

LinkedIn: linkedin.com/in/jparsons
Facebook: facebook.com/parsonscoaching

Best of luck with your Job Search – now go get Hired!

www.ingramcontent.com/pod-product-compliance
Lightning Source LLC
Chambersburg PA
CBHW070458220526
45466CB00004B/1876